Romeo Explores
THE CITY

Romeo Explores
THE CITY

ALAIN GRÉE

Button BOOKS

Romeo the dog loves exploring. Wherever he goes,
he wants to find out more about the world around him.

Would you like to help Romeo explore? On every page he will ask a question about what he sees in the city. See if you can think of the answer then turn the page to check if you are right.

What vehicle looks like a red lorry with a ladder on top?

A fire engine

Where do we go when we want to travel by plane?

An airport

What do we call
the train system that
travels under the city?

The underground

Northbound

NEWSPAPERS

FLOWERS

Northbound

15

Southbound

ETS

Southbound

ROMEO

What goes round
and round with
happy children on it?

A carousel

What do we call a
car that stops when
you wave it down?

A taxi

Where do people go when they need to catch a train?

The train station

Central Station

What do we call the place where we can see lots of different animals?

The zoo

LIONS

TIGERS

BEARS

Where do we go when we want to buy toys or clothes?

The shops

What has stripes and is used to walk across the road safely?

A zebra crossing

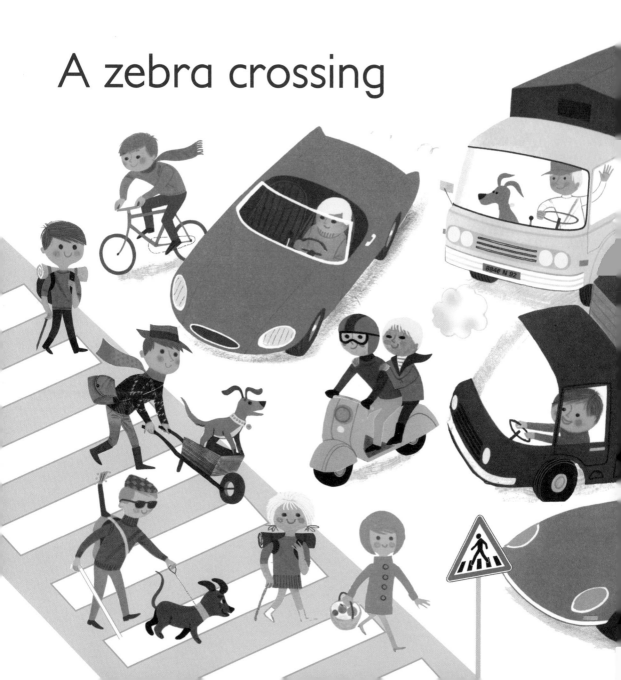

Well done! With your help, Romeo has explored the city and found out all about it. Where shall we explore next?